the epistles of paul the apostle to the

corinthians

authorised king james version

printed by authority

published by canongate

with an introduction by | fay weldon

First published in Great Britain in 1998
by Canongate Books Ltd
14 High Street, Edinburgh EH1 1TE

10 9 8 7 6 5 4 3 2

Introduction copyright © Fay Weldon 1998
The moral right of the author has been asserted

British Library Cataloguing-in-Publication Data
A catalogue record is available on request from
the British Library

ISBN 0 86241 799 6

Typeset by Palimpsest Book Production
Book design by Paddy Cramsie
Printed and bound in Great Britain
by Caledonian International, Bishopbriggs

a note about pocket canons

The Authorised King James Version of the Bible, translated between 1603–11, coincided with an extraordinary flowering of English literature. This version, more than any other, and possibly more than any other work in history, has had an influence in shaping the language we speak and write today. Presenting individual books from the Bible as separate volumes, as they were originally conceived, encourages the reader to approach them as literary works in their own right.

The first twelve books in this series encompass categories as diverse as history, fiction, philosophy, love poetry and law. Each Pocket Canon also has its own introduction, specially commissioned from an impressive range of writers, which provides a personal interpretation of the text and explores its contemporary relevance.

Fay Weldon was born in England and raised in New Zealand. She took degrees in Economics and Psychology at the University of St Andrews in Scotland and then, after a decade of odd jobs and hard times, began writing fiction. She is now well known as novelist, screenwriter and cultural journalist. Her novels include The Life and Loves of a She-Devil *(a major movie starring Meryl Streep and Roseanne Barr),* Puffball, The Cloning of Joanna May, Affliction *and* Worst Fears. *She is the writer of Channel 4's successful series* Big Women, *and has several collections of short stories to her name, in particular* A Hard Time to be a Father. *She has four sons and lives in London.*

introduction by fay weldon

It is hard to *like* Paul the Apostle. One is not out of sympathy when Ananias the Chief Priest of Jerusalem tries to get him thrown out of town for preaching the Christian gospel and remarks to the Roman authorities, 'We have found him a pestilent fellow'. There seems to be so little love flowing from Paul, other than 'in God' which sometimes seems a way of getting out of the need for it in person, and perhaps why so many cruelties get to be perpetrated in God's name. Certainly, all, at the time, were in awe of this slippery, preaching, threatening, cajoling young man, always one step ahead of his enemies: he who BC would have been a prophet but AD must be an apostle, he who has a hot-line to God and God to him (or so he says), but *like* him? No. Many at the time must have suspected that on the road to Damascus this turncoat Paul, once Saul the persecutor of the Christians, did not see God, but rather a path to personal power, twinkling and beckoning in the desert sun. Perhaps Paul the Apostle simply 'crossed the floor' in the political parlance of our own country, our own age. When all of a sudden it seems the other side is singing the best tunes, over you go. Why hang around? Enemy becomes friend, and vice versa.

Prating 'love', this Apostle Paul rants, rails, reproaches and leads others into mortal danger, preaching the forbidden gospel. Letters to the little groups of Christians, digging in here and there – Corinthia, Galatia, Ephesia, Rome itself – model for all revolutionary movements thereafter, confirming them in their dangerous belief. At the time, 'Behold, I see the heavens opened and the Son of Man standing on the right hand of God' was a statement sufficiently bold to get poor Stephen – 'a man full of faith and the Holy Ghost' – brought before Saul and stoned to death. That was our Saul before Damascus, that was, before he changed his name to Paul; our Saul in full scourging flight, 'breathing out threatenings and slaughter against the disciples of the Lord'. Does the leopard change his spots as he changes sides?

And doesn't Paul take up such an annoyingly large chunk of the Bible, after the romance and passion and savagery of the early days are all finished, after that death upon the cross, with his undramatic letters to here and letters to there? A very Mandelson of religious politics, demanding his united front? Listen to Paul in *Corinthians*. 'Now I beseech you, brethren, by the name of our Lord, that ye all speak the same thing, and that there be no divisions amongst you, but that you be perfectly joined together in the same judgement.' Oh, thanks! And it's to be *your* judgement, isn't it, because you have the hot-line to God? Or say you have. Don't smoke, don't own guns, don't be unrighteous, don't spit in church, let's have no dissension here! Don't, don't, don't. Put away our adulthood and submit – be as a little child. 'For now we see as in a glass, darkly, but then face to face.' How quickly the early church, under Paul's tuition, ceases to be visionary and turns respectable. How short are the days of miracle and wonder. Believe, behave! Consult, unite! We're under threat here, and how many divisions did the intellectuals ever have? Ignore them. 'For it is written I will destroy the wisdom of the wise.'

Judgement is nothing, you men and women of Corinthia, clustering together in your ochre landscape, your rough dwellings squatting low upon the burning land. The spirit is all, and the new faith. And what hope this new faith brings. Life is not so short, and brutish and hard as you thought: only believe and you are saved, the Kingdom of God is at hand: oh fortunate generation, with the marvel of the coming of the Son of Man still in living memory.

Though Paul your Apostle never actually met Him face to face he has talked to those who have, and God himself has appeared to Paul once or twice, and sent an Angel to free him from prison (the two gaolers were put to death as a consequence, which always seemed unfair). The Holy Ghost is a familiar visitor too, bringing with him the gift of tongues, the word of God (so long as you can un-garble it), that same gift which charismatic sects still experience today. Though not so terrifying as once it was, the descent of the Holy Spirit is diminished in these cosy days into something seen rather as a relaxing kind of psychotherapy – or else defined as glossolalia, the mere description of a medical condition.

Love is all, writes Paul, so long of course as it's 'in God' and not in the flesh. 'Marry or burn!' (What a master of the sound-bite is this Paul!) Spare us from fornication, for the flesh can only exist at the expense of the spirit, so the flesh must be subdued, a doctrine which has suited many ever since.

'It is good for a man not to touch a woman,' says Paul and can it be that as a result of these eleven words for near on two thousand years women have been seen as temptation, and blamed, and priests have been celibate, and miserable (or gay) and sex a source of so much shame and degradation? Are men and women so easily led? So easily persuaded to forgo pleasure for the sake of principle? It seems so. Better to be as he himself is, says Paul, and celibate, but if you can't help it, then marry and behave. At least Paul has this much mercy: perhaps he saw the impracticality of what he wanted to achieve: a world without sex. 'Let the husband render unto the wife due benevolence: and likewise also the wife unto the husband.' Well, that's okay. That's generous, that's civilised, that's better than many manage or preach today, let alone then. Kindness and good manners get us a long way.

And next to sex there's bad company. 'Adulterers and effeminates: revilers and abusers of themselves with mankind.' Abhor, abjure! 'A fornicator, or covetous, or an idolater, or a railer, or a drunkard, or an extortioner: with such a one, no, not to eat.' Well, that makes sense. My mother, aged ninety, assures me that the breakdown of family life began on the first occasion a person declared guilty in a divorce case was asked to dinner. Forget when they got allowed into the Royal Enclosure at Ascot. Yes, folks, there was a time when moral blame was levelled at those who erred in sexual matters: when the breakdown of a marriage meant one party was guilty and one was innocent and the Court was prepared to say which. Nowadays there's simply no time for any of that. But who is to say we were not happier then?

And yet because we today don't much like Paul, it does not mean God was not speaking to him. The ways of the Creator are very strange. Our contemporary judgement, our political, emotional and spiritual correctnesses are not His. The magic of the language of Corinthians must be our evidence as to the actuality or otherwise of revelation. Did the Paul we know write the words? Or did the angels, as he claimed, write through him? Write, not speak, I say advisedly, for every writer knows the moment when the words on the page seem driven not by the mind but by an understanding that they already exist and which the hand merely serves. Remember that these are actual letters, written on parchment rolls, laboriously. They are not, unlike the rest of the Bible, spoken words of myth, fable and history mixed, flowing through a dusty landscape, gathered together from a thousand doubtful sources and recorded by those who often had their own interest to serve. They come from the hand of the writer, and can of course change in translation but that's about all.

'Though I speak with the tongues of men and angels,' writes St Paul the poet, 'and have not charity, I am become sounding brass or tinkling cymbal. And though I have the gift of prophecy and understand all mysteries and all knowledge: and though I have all faith, so I could remove mountains, and have not charity, I am nothing … Charity suffereth long and is kind: charity envieth not: charity vaunteth not itself, is not puffed up ... Doth not behave itself unseemly, seeketh not her own: is not easily provoked, thinketh no evil ...' We all know the passage, and rightly, for it is part of our Christian heritage, even if only to be spoken to us warningly by teachers. (I suspect Kipling based his poem *If* upon 2 *Corinthians* 1:13.)

'Charity' is often translated as 'love', but that word too has become so misused it begins to lose grandeur. The original word derives from the Roman *caritas*, usually translated as 'affection' but that too in context lacks gravitas. Our new 'empathy' is probably nearer to the actual meaning, but who could use such a base and modern word for so magnificent a usage? What is meant, I think, by 'charity' is the unexpected lurch of the heart towards others which can take the soul by surprise. So that 'now abideth faith, hope and charity, and the greatest of these is charity,' and if Paul, apostate and poet, tells us so, we had better believe him. The timeless truths remain. Two millennia are just the twinkling of an eye in the sight of God, and/or the writer.

the first epistle of paul the apostle to the corinthians

Paul, called to be an apostle of Jesus Christ through the will of God, and Sosthenes our brother, ² unto the church of God which is at Corinth, to them that are sanctified in Christ Jesus, called to be saints, with all that in every place call upon the name of Jesus Christ our Lord, both theirs and ours: ³ Grace be unto you, and peace, from God our Father, and from the Lord Jesus Christ.

⁴ I thank my God always on your behalf, for the grace of God which is given you by Jesus Christ: ⁵ that in every thing ye are enriched by him, in all utterance, and in all knowledge, ⁶ even as the testimony of Christ was confirmed in you, ⁷ so that ye come behind in no gift; waiting for the coming of our Lord Jesus Christ, ⁸ who shall also confirm you unto the end, that ye may be blameless in the day of our Lord Jesus Christ. ⁹ God is faithful, by whom ye were called unto the fellowship of his Son Jesus Christ our Lord.

¹⁰ Now I beseech you, brethren, by the name of our Lord Jesus Christ, that ye all speak the same thing, and that there be no divisions among you, but that ye be perfectly joined together in the same mind and in the same judgment. ¹¹ For it hath been declared unto me of you, my brethren, by them which are of the house of Chloe, that there are contentions

among you. ¹²Now this I say, that every one of you saith, 'I am of Paul,' and 'I of Apollos,' and 'I of Cephas,' and 'I of Christ.' ¹³Is Christ divided? Was Paul crucified for you? Or were ye baptized in the name of Paul? ¹⁴I thank God that I baptized none of you, but Crispus and Gaius, ¹⁵lest any should say that I had baptized in mine own name. ¹⁶And I baptized also the household of Stephanas; besides, I know not whether I baptized any other. ¹⁷For Christ sent me not to baptize, but to preach the gospel: not with wisdom of words, lest the cross of Christ should be made of none effect.

¹⁸For the preaching of the cross is to them that perish foolishness, but unto us which are saved it is the power of God. ¹⁹For it is written, 'I will destroy the wisdom of the wise, and will bring to nothing the understanding of the prudent.' ²⁰Where is the wise? Where is the scribe? Where is the disputer of this world? Hath not God made foolish the wisdom of this world? ²¹For after that in the wisdom of God the world by wisdom knew not God, it pleased God by the foolishness of preaching to save them that believe. ²²For the Jews require a sign, and the Greeks seek after wisdom, ²³but we preach Christ crucified, unto the Jews a stumbling-block, and unto the Greeks foolishness, ²⁴but unto them which are called, both Jews and Greeks, Christ the power of God, and the wisdom of God. ²⁵Because the foolishness of God is wiser than men; and the weakness of God is stronger than men.

²⁶For ye see your calling, brethren, how that not many wise men after the flesh, not many mighty, not many noble, are called, ²⁷but God hath chosen the foolish things of the world to confound the wise; and God hath chosen the weak

things of the world to confound the things which are mighty; [28] and base things of the world, and things which are despised, hath God chosen, yea, and things which are not, to bring to nought things that are, [29] that no flesh should glory in his presence. [30] But of him are ye in Christ Jesus, who of God is made unto us wisdom, and righteousness, and sanctification, and redemption, [31] that, according as it is written, 'He that glorieth, let him glory in the Lord.'

2 And I, brethren, when I came to you, came not with excellency of speech or of wisdom, declaring unto you the testimony of God. [2] For I determined not to know any thing among you, save Jesus Christ, and him crucified. [3] And I was with you in weakness, and in fear, and in much trembling. [4] And my speech and my preaching was not with enticing words of man's wisdom, but in demonstration of the Spirit and of power, [5] that your faith should not stand in the wisdom of men, but in the power of God.

[6] Howbeit we speak wisdom among them that are perfect: yet not the wisdom of this world, nor of the princes of this world, that come to nought; [7] but we speak the wisdom of God in a mystery, even the hidden wisdom, which God ordained before the world unto our glory, [8] which none of the princes of this world knew, for had they known it, they would not have crucified the Lord of glory. [9] But as it is written, 'Eye hath not seen, nor ear heard, neither have entered into the heart of man, the things which God hath prepared for them that love him.' [10] But God hath revealed them unto us by his Spirit, for the Spirit searcheth all things, yea, the

deep things of God. ¹¹ For what man knoweth the things of a man, save the spirit of man which is in him? Even so the things of God knoweth no man, but the Spirit of God. ¹² Now we have received, not the spirit of the world, but the spirit which is of God, that we might know the things that are freely given to us of God. ¹³ Which things also we speak, not in the words which man's wisdom teacheth, but which the Holy Ghost teacheth; comparing spiritual things with spiritual.

¹⁴ But the natural man receiveth not the things of the Spirit of God, for they are foolishness unto him; neither can he know them, because they are spiritually discerned. ¹⁵ But he that is spiritual judgeth all things, yet he himself is judged of no man. ¹⁶ 'For who hath known the mind of the Lord, that he may instruct him?' But we have the mind of Christ.

3 And I, brethren, could not speak unto you as unto spiritual, but as unto carnal, even as unto babes in Christ. ² I have fed you with milk, and not with meat, for hitherto ye were not able to bear it, neither yet now are ye able. ³ For ye are yet carnal, for whereas there is among you envying, and strife, and divisions, are ye not carnal, and walk as men? ⁴ For while one saith, 'I am of Paul,' and another, 'I am of Apollos,' are ye not carnal?

⁵ Who then is Paul, and who is Apollos, but ministers by whom ye believed, even as the Lord gave to every man? ⁶ I have planted, Apollos watered; but God gave the increase. ⁷ So then neither is he that planteth any thing, neither he that watereth; but God that giveth the increase. ⁸ Now he that planteth and he that watereth are one, and every man shall

receive his own reward according to his own labour. ⁹For we are labourers together with God; ye are God's husbandry, ye are God's building.

¹⁰According to the grace of God which is given unto me, as a wise masterbuilder, I have laid the foundation, and another buildeth thereon. But let every man take heed how he buildeth thereupon. ¹¹For other foundation can no man lay than that is laid, which is Jesus Christ. ¹²Now if any man build upon this foundation gold, silver, precious stones, wood, hay, stubble, ¹³every man's work shall be made manifest, for the day shall declare it, because it shall be revealed by fire; and the fire shall try every man's work of what sort it is. ¹⁴If any man's work abide which he hath built thereupon, he shall receive a reward. ¹⁵If any man's work shall be burned, he shall suffer loss, but he himself shall be saved; yet so as by fire.

¹⁶Know ye not that ye are the temple of God, and that the Spirit of God dwelleth in you? ¹⁷If any man defile the temple of God, him shall God destroy, for the temple of God is holy, which temple ye are. ¹⁸Let no man deceive himself. If any man among you seemeth to be wise in this world, let him become a fool, that he may be wise. ¹⁹For the wisdom of this world is foolishness with God. For it is written, 'He taketh the wise in their own craftiness,' ²⁰and again, 'The Lord knoweth the thoughts of the wise, that they are vain.' ²¹Therefore let no man glory in men. For all things are yours, ²²whether Paul, or Apollos, or Cephas, or the world, or life, or death, or things present, or things to come; all are yours; ²³and ye are Christ's; and Christ is God's.

4 Let a man so account of us, as of the ministers of Christ, and stewards of the mysteries of God. ²Moreover it is required in stewards, that a man be found faithful. ³But with me it is a very small thing that I should be judged of you, or of man's judgment; yea, I judge not mine own self. ⁴For I know nothing by myself; yet am I not hereby justified; but he that judgeth me is the Lord. ⁵Therefore judge nothing before the time, until the Lord come, who both will bring to light the hidden things of darkness, and will make manifest the counsels of the hearts, and then shall every man have praise of God.

⁶And these things, brethren, I have in a figure transferred to myself and to Apollos for your sakes; that ye might learn in us not to think of men above that which is written, that no one of you be puffed up for one against another. ⁷For who maketh thee to differ from another? And what hast thou that thou didst not receive? Now if thou didst receive it, why dost thou glory, as if thou hadst not received it?

⁸Now ye are full, now ye are rich, ye have reigned as kings without us, and I would to God ye did reign, that we also might reign with you. ⁹For I think that God hath set forth us the apostles last, as it were appointed to death, for we are made a spectacle unto the world, and to angels, and to men. ¹⁰We are fools for Christ's sake, but ye are wise in Christ; we are weak, but ye are strong; ye are honourable, but we are despised. ¹¹Even unto this present hour we both hunger, and thirst, and are naked, and are buffeted, and have no certain dwellingplace; ¹²and labour, working with our own hands. Being reviled, we bless; being persecuted, we

suffer it; ¹³ being defamed, we intreat. We are made as the filth of the world, and are the offscouring of all things unto this day.

¹⁴ I write not these things to shame you, but as my beloved sons I warn you. ¹⁵ For though ye have ten thousand instructers in Christ, yet have ye not many fathers, for in Christ Jesus I have begotten you through the gospel. ¹⁶ Wherefore I beseech you, be ye followers of me. ¹⁷ For this cause have I sent unto you Timotheus, who is my beloved son, and faithful in the Lord, who shall bring you into remembrance of my ways which be in Christ, as I teach every where in every church. ¹⁸ Now some are puffed up, as though I would not come to you. ¹⁹ But I will come to you shortly, if the Lord will, and will know, not the speech of them which are puffed up, but the power. ²⁰ For the kingdom of God is not in word, but in power. ²¹ What will ye? Shall I come unto you with a rod, or in love, and in the spirit of meekness?

5 It is reported commonly that there is fornication among you, and such fornication as is not so much as named among the Gentiles, that one should have his father's wife. ² And ye are puffed up, and have not rather mourned, that he that hath done this deed might be taken away from among you.

³ For I verily, as absent in body, but present in spirit, have judged already, as though I were present, concerning him that hath so done this deed, ⁴ in the name of our Lord Jesus Christ, when ye are gathered together, and my spirit, with the power of our Lord Jesus Christ, ⁵ to deliver such an one

unto Satan for the destruction of the flesh, that the spirit may be saved in the day of the Lord Jesus.

⁶ Your glorying is not good. Know ye not that a little leaven leaveneth the whole lump? ⁷ Purge out therefore the old leaven, that ye may be a new lump, as ye are unleavened. For even Christ our passover is sacrificed for us; ⁸ therefore let us keep the feast, not with old leaven, neither with the leaven of malice and wickedness, but with the unleavened bread of sincerity and truth.

⁹ I wrote unto you in an epistle not to company with fornicators; ¹⁰ yet not altogether with the fornicators of this world, or with the covetous, or extortioners, or with idolaters, for then must ye needs go out of the world. ¹¹ But now I have written unto you not to keep company, if any man that is called a brother be a fornicator, or covetous, or an idolater, or a railer, or a drunkard, or an extortioner; with such an one no not to eat. ¹² For what have I to do to judge them also that are without? Do not ye judge them that are within? ¹³ But them that are without God judgeth. Therefore put away from among yourselves that wicked person.

6 Dare any of you, having a matter against another, go to law before the unjust, and not before the saints? ² Do ye not know that the saints shall judge the world? And if the world shall be judged by you, are ye unworthy to judge the smallest matters? ³ Know ye not that we shall judge angels? How much more things that pertain to this life? ⁴ If then ye have judgments of things pertaining to this life, set them to judge who are least esteemed in the church. ⁵ I speak to your

shame. Is it so, that there is not a wise man among you? No, not one that shall be able to judge between his brethren? 6 But brother goeth to law with brother, and that before the unbelievers.

7 Now therefore there is utterly a fault among you, because ye go to law one with another. Why do ye not rather take wrong? Why do ye not rather suffer yourselves to be defrauded? 8 Nay, ye do wrong, and defraud, and that your brethren.

9 Know ye not that the unrighteous shall not inherit the kingdom of God? Be not deceived: neither fornicators, nor idolaters, nor adulterers, nor effeminate, nor abusers of themselves with mankind, 10 nor thieves, nor covetous, nor drunkards, nor revilers, nor extortioners, shall inherit the kingdom of God. 11 And such were some of you: but ye are washed, but ye are sanctified, but ye are justified in the name of the Lord Jesus, and by the Spirit of our God.

12 All things are lawful unto me, but all things are not expedient; all things are lawful for me, but I will not be brought under the power of any. 13 Meats for the belly, and the belly for meats, but God shall destroy both it and them. Now the body is not for fornication, but for the Lord; and the Lord for the body. 14 And God hath both raised up the Lord, and will also raise up us by his own power. 15 Know ye not that your bodies are the members of Christ? Shall I then take the members of Christ, and make them the members of an harlot? God forbid. 16 What? Know ye not that he which is joined to an harlot is one body? For two, saith he, shall be one flesh. 17 But he that is joined unto the Lord is one spirit.

[18] Flee fornication. Every sin that a man doeth is without the body, but he that committeth fornication sinneth against his own body. [19] What? Know ye not that your body is the temple of the Holy Ghost which is in you, which ye have of God, and ye are not your own? [20] For ye are bought with a price; therefore glorify God in your body, and in your spirit, which are God's.

7 Now concerning the things whereof ye wrote unto me: 'It is good for a man not to touch a woman.' [2] Nevertheless, to avoid fornication, let every man have his own wife, and let every woman have her own husband. [3] Let the husband render unto the wife due benevolence, and likewise also the wife unto the husband. [4] The wife hath not power of her own body, but the husband, and likewise also the husband hath not power of his own body, but the wife. [5] Defraud ye not one the other, except it be with consent for a time, that ye may give yourselves to fasting and prayer; and come together again, that Satan tempt you not for your incontinency. [6] But I speak this by permission, and not of commandment. [7] For I would that all men were even as I myself. But every man hath his proper gift of God, one after this manner, and another after that.

[8] I say therefore to the unmarried and widows: it is good for them if they abide even as I. [9] But if they cannot contain, let them marry, for it is better to marry than to burn.

[10] And unto the married I command, yet not I, but the Lord, let not the wife depart from her husband; [11] but and if she depart, let her remain unmarried, or be reconciled to her

husband, and let not the husband put away his wife.

¹² But to the rest speak I, not the Lord: if any brother hath a wife that believeth not, and she be pleased to dwell with him, let him not put her away. ¹³ And the woman which hath an husband that believeth not, and if he be pleased to dwell with her, let her not leave him. ¹⁴ For the unbelieving husband is sanctified by the wife, and the unbelieving wife is sanctified by the husband: else were your children unclean; but now are they holy. ¹⁵ But if the unbelieving depart, let him depart. A brother or a sister is not under bondage in such cases, but God hath called us to peace. ¹⁶ For what knowest thou, O wife, whether thou shalt save thy husband? Or how knowest thou, O man, whether thou shalt save thy wife?

¹⁷ But as God hath distributed to every man, as the Lord hath called every one, so let him walk. And so ordain I in all churches. ¹⁸ Is any man called being circumcised? Let him not become uncircumcised. Is any called in uncircumcision? Let him not be circumcised. ¹⁹ Circumcision is nothing, and uncircumcision is nothing, but the keeping of the commandments of God. ²⁰ Let every man abide in the same calling wherein he was called.

²¹ Art thou called being a servant? Care not for it, but if thou mayest be made free, use it rather. ²² For he that is called in the Lord, being a servant, is the Lord's freeman; likewise also he that is called, being free, is Christ's servant. ²³ Ye are bought with a price; be not ye the servants of men. ²⁴ Brethren, let every man, wherein he is called, therein abide with God.

²⁵ Now concerning virgins I have no commandment of the Lord; yet I give my judgment, as one that hath obtained

mercy of the Lord to be faithful. ²⁶ I suppose therefore that this is good for the present distress, I say, that it is good for a man so to be. ²⁷ Art thou bound unto a wife? Seek not to be loosed. Art thou loosed from a wife? Seek not a wife. ²⁸ But and if thou marry, thou hast not sinned; and if a virgin marry, she hath not sinned. Nevertheless such shall have trouble in the flesh, but I spare you. ²⁹ But this I say, brethren, the time is short: it remaineth, that both they that have wives be as though they had none; ³⁰ and they that weep, as though they wept not; and they that rejoice, as though they rejoiced not; and they that buy, as though they possessed not; ³¹ and they that use this world, as not abusing it; for the fashion of this world passeth away.

³² But I would have you without carefulness. He that is unmarried careth for the things that belong to the Lord, how he may please the Lord, ³³ but he that is married careth for the things that are of the world, how he may please his wife. ³⁴ There is difference also between a wife and a virgin. The unmarried woman careth for the things of the Lord, that she may be holy both in body and in spirit, but she that is married careth for the things of the world, how she may please her husband. ³⁵ And this I speak for your own profit; not that I may cast a snare upon you, but for that which is comely, and that ye may attend upon the Lord without distraction.

³⁶ But if any man think that he behaveth himself uncomely toward his virgin, if she pass the flower of her age, and need so require, let him do what he will, he sinneth not: let them marry. ³⁷ Nevertheless he that standeth stedfast in his heart, having no necessity, but hath power over his own will, and

hath so decreed in his heart that he will keep his virgin, doeth well. ³⁸ So then he that giveth her in marriage doeth well; but he that giveth her not in marriage doeth better.

³⁹ The wife is bound by the law as long as her husband liveth; but if her husband be dead, she is at liberty to be married to whom she will; only in the Lord. ⁴⁰ But she is happier if she so abide, after my judgment, and I think also that I have the Spirit of God.

8 Now as touching things offered unto idols, we know that we all have knowledge. Knowledge puffeth up, but charity edifieth. ²And if any man think that he knoweth any thing, he knoweth nothing yet as he ought to know. ³But if any man love God, the same is known of him.

⁴As concerning therefore the eating of those things that are offered in sacrifice unto idols, we know that an idol is nothing in the world, and that there is none other God but one. ⁵For though there be that are called gods, whether in heaven or in earth (as there be gods many, and lords many), ⁶but to us there is but one God, the Father, of whom are all things, and we in him, and one Lord Jesus Christ, by whom are all things, and we by him.

⁷Howbeit there is not in every man that knowledge, for some with conscience of the idol unto this hour eat it as a thing offered unto an idol; and their conscience being weak is defiled. ⁸But meat commendeth us not to God: for neither, if we eat, are we the better; neither, if we eat not, are we the worse. ⁹But take heed lest by any means this liberty of yours become a stumbling-block to them that are weak. ¹⁰For if any

man see thee which hast knowledge sit at meat in the idol's temple, shall not the conscience of him which is weak be emboldened to eat those things which are offered to idols, ¹¹and through thy knowledge shall the weak brother perish, for whom Christ died? ¹²But when ye sin so against the brethren, and wound their weak conscience, ye sin against Christ. ¹³Wherefore, if meat make my brother to offend, I will eat no flesh while the world standeth, lest I make my brother to offend.

9 Am I not an apostle? Am I not free? Have I not seen Jesus Christ our Lord? Are not ye my work in the Lord? ²If I be not an apostle unto others, yet doubtless I am to you, for the seal of mine apostleship are ye in the Lord.

³Mine answer to them that do examine me is this. ⁴Have we not power to eat and to drink? ⁵Have we not power to lead about a sister, a wife, as well as other apostles, and as the brethren of the Lord, and Cephas? ⁶Or I only and Barnabas, have not we power to forbear working? ⁷Who goeth a warfare any time at his own charges? Who planteth a vineyard, and eateth not of the fruit thereof? Or who feedeth a flock, and eateth not of the milk of the flock?

⁸Say I these things as a man? Or saith not the law the same also? ⁹For it is written in the law of Moses, 'Thou shalt not muzzle the mouth of the ox that treadeth out the corn.' Doth God take care for oxen? ¹⁰Or saith he it altogether for our sakes? For our sakes, no doubt, this is written: 'That he that ploweth should plow in hope, and that he that thresheth in hope should be partaker of his hope.' ¹¹If we have

sown unto you spiritual things, is it a great thing if we shall reap your carnal things? ¹² If others be partakers of this power over you, are not we rather? Nevertheless we have not used this power; but suffer all things, lest we should hinder the gospel of Christ. ¹³ Do ye not know that they which minister about holy things live of the things of the temple? And they which wait at the altar are partakers with the altar? ¹⁴ Even so hath the Lord ordained that they which preach the gospel should live of the gospel.

¹⁵ But I have used none of these things; neither have I written these things, that it should be so done unto me, for it were better for me to die, than that any man should make my glorying void. ¹⁶ For though I preach the gospel, I have nothing to glory of, for necessity is laid upon me; yea, woe is unto me, if I preach not the gospel! ¹⁷ For if I do this thing willingly, I have a reward, but if against my will, a dispensation of the gospel is committed unto me. ¹⁸ What is my reward then? Verily that, when I preach the gospel, I may make the gospel of Christ without charge, that I abuse not my power in the gospel.

¹⁹ For though I be free from all men, yet have I made myself servant unto all, that I might gain the more. ²⁰ And unto the Jews I became as a Jew, that I might gain the Jews; to them that are under the law, as under the law, that I might gain them that are under the law; ²¹ to them that are without law, as without law (being not without law to God, but under the law to Christ), that I might gain them that are without law. ²² To the weak became I as weak, that I might gain the weak. I am made all things to all men, that I might by all

means save some. ²³And this I do for the gospel's sake, that I might be partaker thereof with you.

²⁴Know ye not that they which run in a race run all, but one receiveth the prize? So run, that ye may obtain. ²⁵And every man that striveth for the mastery is temperate in all things. Now they do it to obtain a corruptible crown, but we an incorruptible. ²⁶I therefore so run, not as uncertainly; so fight I, not as one that beateth the air, ²⁷but I keep under my body, and bring it into subjection, lest that by any means, when I have preached to others, I myself should be a castaway.

10 Moreover, brethren, I would not that ye should be ignorant, how that all our fathers were under the cloud, and all passed through the sea, ²and were all baptized unto Moses in the cloud and in the sea, ³and did all eat the same spiritual meat, ⁴and did all drink the same spiritual drink, for they drank of that spiritual Rock that followed them, and that Rock was Christ. ⁵But with many of them God was not well pleased, for they were overthrown in the wilderness.

⁶Now these things were our examples, to the intent we should not lust after evil things, as they also lusted. ⁷Neither be ye idolaters, as were some of them; as it is written, 'The people sat down to eat and drink, and rose up to play.' ⁸Neither let us commit fornication, as some of them committed, and fell in one day three and twenty thousand. ⁹Neither let us tempt Christ, as some of them also tempted, and were destroyed of serpents. ¹⁰Neither murmur ye, as some of them

also murmured, and were destroyed of the destroyer. ¹¹ Now all these things happened unto them for ensamples, and they are written for our admonition, upon whom the ends of the world are come. ¹² Wherefore let him that thinketh he standeth take heed lest he fall. ¹³ There hath no temptation taken you but such as is common to man, but God is faithful, who will not suffer you to be tempted above that ye are able, but will with the temptation also make a way to escape, that ye may be able to bear it.

¹⁴ Wherefore, my dearly beloved, flee from idolatry. ¹⁵ I speak as to wise men; judge ye what I say. ¹⁶ The cup of blessing which we bless, is it not the communion of the blood of Christ? The bread which we break, is it not the communion of the body of Christ? ¹⁷ For we being many are one bread, and one body, for we are all partakers of that one bread. ¹⁸ Behold Israel after the flesh: are not they which eat of the sacrifices partakers of the altar? ¹⁹ What say I then? That the idol is any thing, or that which is offered in sacrifice to idols is any thing? ²⁰ But I say, that the things which the Gentiles sacrifice, they sacrifice to devils, and not to God, and I would not that ye should have fellowship with devils. ²¹ Ye cannot drink the cup of the Lord, and the cup of devils; ye cannot be partakers of the Lord's table, and of the table of devils. ²² Do we provoke the Lord to jealousy? Are we stronger than he?

²³ All things are lawful for me, but all things are not expedient; all things are lawful for me, but all things edify not. ²⁴ Let no man seek his own, but every man another's wealth. ²⁵ Whatsoever is sold in the shambles, that eat, asking no question for conscience sake, ²⁶ for the earth is the Lord's, and

the fulness thereof. ²⁷ If any of them that believe not bid you to a feast, and ye be disposed to go; whatsoever is set before you, eat, asking no question for conscience sake. ²⁸ But if any man say unto you, 'This is offered in sacrifice unto idols,' eat not for his sake that shewed it, and for conscience sake, for the earth is the Lord's, and the fulness thereof. ²⁹ Conscience, I say, not thine own, but of the other: for why is my liberty judged of another man's conscience? ³⁰ For if I by grace be a partaker, why am I evil spoken of for that for which I give thanks?

³¹ Whether therefore ye eat, or drink, or whatsoever ye do, do all to the glory of God. ³² Give none offence, neither to the Jews, nor to the Gentiles, nor to the church of God. ³³ Even as I please all men in all things, not seeking mine own profit, but the profit of many, that they may be saved.

11 Be ye followers of me, even as I also am of Christ. ² Now I praise you, brethren, that ye remember me in all things, and keep the ordinances, as I delivered them to you. ³ But I would have you know that the head of every man is Christ; and the head of the woman is the man; and the head of Christ is God. ⁴ Every man praying or prophesying, having his head covered, dishonoureth his head. ⁵ But every woman that prayeth or prophesieth with her head uncovered dishonoureth her head, for that is even all one as if she were shaven. ⁶ For if the woman be not covered, let her also be shorn, but if it be a shame for a woman to be shorn or shaven, let her be covered. ⁷ For a man indeed ought not to cover his head, forasmuch as he is the image and glory of

God, but the woman is the glory of the man. ⁸For the man is not of the woman, but the woman of the man. ⁹Neither was the man created for the woman, but the woman for the man. ¹⁰For this cause ought the woman to have power on her head because of the angels. ¹¹Nevertheless neither is the man without the woman, neither the woman without the man, in the Lord. ¹²For as the woman is of the man, even so is the man also by the woman; but all things of God. ¹³Judge in yourselves: is it comely that a woman pray unto God uncovered? ¹⁴Doth not even nature itself teach you, that, if a man have long hair, it is a shame unto him? ¹⁵But if a woman have long hair, it is a glory to her, for her hair is given her for a covering. ¹⁶But if any man seem to be contentious, we have no such custom, neither the churches of God.

¹⁷Now in this that I declare unto you I praise you not, that ye come together not for the better, but for the worse. ¹⁸For first of all, when ye come together in the church, I hear that there be divisions among you; and I partly believe it. ¹⁹For there must be also heresies among you, that they which are approved may be made manifest among you. ²⁰When ye come together therefore into one place, this is not to eat the Lord's supper. ²¹For in eating every one taketh before other his own supper, and one is hungry, and another is drunken. ²²What? Have ye not houses to eat and to drink in? Or despise ye the church of God, and shame them that have not? What shall I say to you? Shall I praise you in this? I praise you not.

²³For I have received of the Lord that which also I delivered unto you, that the Lord Jesus the same night in which

he was betrayed took bread, ²⁴ and when he had given thanks, he brake it, and said, 'Take, eat; this is my body, which is broken for you; this do in remembrance of me.' ²⁵ After the same manner also he took the cup, when he had supped, saying, 'This cup is the new testament in my blood; this do ye, as oft as ye drink it, in remembrance of me.' ²⁶ For as often as ye eat this bread, and drink this cup, ye do shew the Lord's death till he come.

²⁷ Wherefore whosoever shall eat this bread, and drink this cup of the Lord, unworthily, shall be guilty of the body and blood of the Lord. ²⁸ But let a man examine himself, and so let him eat of that bread, and drink of that cup. ²⁹ For he that eateth and drinketh unworthily, eateth and drinketh damnation to himself, not discerning the Lord's body. ³⁰ For this cause many are weak and sickly among you, and many sleep. ³¹ For if we would judge ourselves, we should not be judged. ³² But when we are judged, we are chastened of the Lord, that we should not be condemned with the world.

³³ Wherefore, my brethren, when ye come together to eat, tarry one for another. ³⁴ And if any man hunger, let him eat at home; that ye come not together unto condemnation. And the rest will I set in order when I come.

12 Now concerning spiritual gifts, brethren, I would not have you ignorant. ² Ye know that ye were Gentiles, carried away unto these dumb idols, even as ye were led. ³ Wherefore I give you to understand, that no man speaking by the Spirit of God calleth Jesus accursed, and that no man can say that Jesus is the Lord, but by the Holy Ghost.

⁴Now there are diversities of gifts, but the same Spirit. ⁵And there are differences of administrations, but the same Lord. ⁶And there are diversities of operations, but it is the same God which worketh all in all. ⁷But the manifestation of the Spirit is given to every man to profit withal. ⁸For to one is given by the Spirit the word of wisdom; to another the word of knowledge by the same Spirit; ⁹to another faith by the same Spirit; to another the gifts of healing by the same Spirit; ¹⁰to another the working of miracles; to another prophecy; to another discerning of spirits; to another divers kinds of tongues; to another the interpretation of tongues; ¹¹but all these worketh that one and the selfsame Spirit, dividing to every man severally as he will.

¹²For as the body is one, and hath many members, and all the members of that one body, being many, are one body; so also is Christ. ¹³For by one Spirit are we all baptized into one body, whether we be Jews or Gentiles, whether we be bond or free, and have been all made to drink into one Spirit.

¹⁴For the body is not one member, but many. ¹⁵If the foot shall say, 'Because I am not the hand, I am not of the body,' is it therefore not of the body? ¹⁶And if the ear shall say, 'Because I am not the eye, I am not of the body,' is it therefore not of the body? ¹⁷If the whole body were an eye, where were the hearing? If the whole were hearing, where were the smelling? ¹⁸But now hath God set the members every one of them in the body, as it hath pleased him. ¹⁹And if they were all one member, where were the body? ²⁰But now are they many members, yet but one body. ²¹And the eye cannot say unto the hand, I have no need of thee; nor again the head to

the feet, I have no need of you. ²² Nay, much more those members of the body, which seem to be more feeble, are necessary; ²³ and those members of the body, which we think to be less honourable, upon these we bestow more abundant honour; and our uncomely parts have more abundant comeliness. ²⁴ For our comely parts have no need, but God hath tempered the body together, having given more abundant honour to that part which lacked, ²⁵ that there should be no schism in the body, but that the members should have the same care one for another. ²⁶ And whether one member suffer, all the members suffer with it; or one member be honoured, all the members rejoice with it.

²⁷ Now ye are the body of Christ, and members in particular. ²⁸ And God hath set some in the church, first apostles, secondarily prophets, thirdly teachers, after that miracles, then gifts of healings, helps, governments, diversities of tongues. ²⁹ Are all apostles? Are all prophets? Are all teachers? Are all workers of miracles? ³⁰ Have all the gifts of healing? Do all speak with tongues? Do all interpret? ³¹ But covet earnestly the best gifts, and yet shew I unto you a more excellent way.

13 Though I speak with the tongues of men and of angels,
and have not charity,
I am become as sounding brass,
or a tinkling cymbal.
²And though I have the gift of prophecy,
and understand all mysteries, and all knowledge;
and though I have all faith,
so that I could remove mountains,

and have not charity, I am nothing.

³And though I bestow all my goods to feed the poor,
   and though I give my body to be burned,
      and have not charity,
   it profiteth me nothing.
⁴Charity suffereth long, and is kind;
   charity envieth not;
      charity vaunteth not itself, is not puffed up,
⁵doth not behave itself unseemly,
   seeketh not her own, is not easily provoked,
      thinketh no evil;
⁶rejoiceth not in iniquity, but rejoiceth in the truth;
   ⁷beareth all things, believeth all things,
      hopeth all things, endureth all things.
⁸Charity never faileth,
   but whether there be prophecies, they shall fail;
      whether there be tongues,
   they shall cease;
      whether there be knowledge,
   it shall vanish away.
⁹For we know in part, and we prophesy in part.
¹⁰But when that which is perfect is come,
   then that which is in part shall be done away.
¹¹When I was a child, I spake as a child,
   I understood as a child, I thought as a child,
      but when I became a man,
   I put away childish things.
¹²For now we see through a glass, darkly;
   but then face to face.

Now I know in part;
but then shall I know even as also I am known. [13]And now abideth faith, hope, charity, these three;
but the greatest of these is charity.

14 Follow after charity, and desire spiritual gifts, but rather that ye may prophesy. [2]For he that speaketh in an unknown tongue speaketh not unto men, but unto God: for no man understandeth him; howbeit in the spirit he speaketh mysteries. [3]But he that prophesieth speaketh unto men to edification, and exhortation, and comfort. [4]He that speaketh in an unknown tongue edifieth himself, but he that prophesieth edifieth the church. [5]I would that ye all spake with tongues, but rather that ye prophesied: for greater is he that prophesieth than he that speaketh with tongues, except he interpret, that the church may receive edifying.

[6]Now, brethren, if I come unto you speaking with tongues, what shall I profit you, except I shall speak to you either by revelation, or by knowledge, or by prophesying, or by doctrine? [7]And even things without life giving sound, whether pipe or harp, except they give a distinction in the sounds, how shall it be known what is piped or harped? [8]For if the trumpet give an uncertain sound, who shall prepare himself to the battle? [9]So likewise ye, except ye utter by the tongue words easy to be understood, how shall it be known what is spoken? For ye shall speak into the air. [10]There are, it may be, so many kinds of voices in the world, and none of them is without signification. [11]Therefore if I

know not the meaning of the voice, I shall be unto him that speaketh a barbarian, and he that speaketh shall be a barbarian unto me. ¹² Even so ye, forasmuch as ye are zealous of spiritual gifts, seek that ye may excel to the edifying of the church.

¹³ Wherefore let him that speaketh in an unknown tongue pray that he may interpret. ¹⁴ For if I pray in an unknown tongue, my spirit prayeth, but my understanding is unfruitful. ¹⁵ What is it then? I will pray with the spirit, and I will pray with the understanding also; I will sing with the spirit, and I will sing with the understanding also. ¹⁶ Else when thou shalt bless with the spirit, how shall he that occupieth the room of the unlearned say 'Amen' at thy giving of thanks, seeing he understandeth not what thou sayest? ¹⁷ For thou verily givest thanks well, but the other is not edified. ¹⁸ I thank my God, I speak with tongues more than ye all; ¹⁹ yet in the church I had rather speak five words with my understanding, that by my voice I might teach others also, than ten thousand words in an unknown tongue.

²⁰ Brethren, be not children in understanding: howbeit in malice be ye children, but in understanding be men. ²¹ In the law it is written, 'With men of other tongues and other lips will I speak unto this people; and yet for all that will they not hear me,' saith the Lord. ²² Wherefore tongues are for a sign, not to them that believe, but to them that believe not, but prophesying serveth not for them that believe not, but for them which believe. ²³ If therefore the whole church be come together into one place, and all speak with tongues, and there come in those that are unlearned, or unbelievers,

will they not say that ye are mad? ²⁴ But if all prophesy, and there come in one that believeth not, or one unlearned, he is convinced of all, he is judged of all, ²⁵ and thus are the secrets of his heart made manifest; and so falling down on his face he will worship God, and report that God is in you of a truth.

²⁶ How is it then, brethren? When ye come together, every one of you hath a psalm, hath a doctrine, hath a tongue, hath a revelation, hath an interpretation. Let all things be done unto edifying. ²⁷ If any man speak in an unknown tongue, let it be by two, or at the most by three, and that by course; and let one interpret. ²⁸ But if there be no interpreter, let him keep silence in the church; and let him speak to himself, and to God. ²⁹ Let the prophets speak two or three, and let the other judge. ³⁰ If any thing be revealed to another that sitteth by, let the first hold his peace. ³¹ For ye may all prophesy one by one, that all may learn, and all may be comforted. ³² And the spirits of the prophets are subject to the prophets. ³³ For God is not the author of confusion, but of peace, as in all churches of the saints. ³⁴ Let your women keep silence in the churches, for it is not permitted unto them to speak, but they are commanded to be under obedience, as also saith the law. ³⁵ And if they will learn any thing, let them ask their husbands at home, for it is a shame for women to speak in the church. ³⁶ What? Came the word of God out from you? Or came it unto you only?

³⁷ If any man think himself to be a prophet, or spiritual, let him acknowledge that the things that I write unto you are the commandments of the Lord. ³⁸ But if any man be ignorant, let him be ignorant. ³⁹ Wherefore, brethren, covet to

prophesy, and forbid not to speak with tongues. ⁴⁰Let all things be done decently and in order.

15 Moreover, brethren, I declare unto you the gospel which I preached unto you, which also ye have received, and wherein ye stand, ²by which also ye are saved, if ye keep in memory what I preached unto you, unless ye have believed in vain.

³For I delivered unto you first of all that which I also received, how that Christ died for our sins according to the scriptures; ⁴and that he was buried, and that he rose again the third day according to the scriptures, ⁵and that he was seen of Cephas, then of the twelve. ⁶After that, he was seen of above five hundred brethren at once; of whom the greater part remain unto this present, but some are fallen asleep. ⁷After that, he was seen of James; then of all the apostles. ⁸And last of all he was seen of me also, as of one born out of due time. ⁹For I am the least of the apostles, that am not meet to be called an apostle, because I persecuted the church of God. ¹⁰But by the grace of God I am what I am: and his grace which was bestowed upon me was not in vain; but I laboured more abundantly than they all; yet not I, but the grace of God which was with me. ¹¹Therefore whether it were I or they, so we preach, and so ye believed.

¹²Now if Christ be preached that he rose from the dead, how say some among you that there is no resurrection of the dead? ¹³But if there be no resurrection of the dead, then is Christ not risen. ¹⁴And if Christ be not risen, then is our preaching vain, and your faith is also vain. ¹⁵Yea, and we are found

false witnesses of God, because we have testified of God that he raised up Christ, whom he raised not up, if so be that the dead rise not. ¹⁶ For if the dead rise not, then is not Christ raised, ¹⁷and if Christ be not raised, your faith is vain; ye are yet in your sins. ¹⁸ Then they also which are fallen asleep in Christ are perished. ¹⁹ If in this life only we have hope in Christ, we are of all men most miserable.

²⁰ But now is Christ risen from the dead, and become the firstfruits of them that slept. ²¹ For since by man came death, by man came also the resurrection of the dead. ²² For as in Adam all die, even so in Christ shall all be made alive. ²³ But every man in his own order: Christ the firstfruits; afterward they that are Christ's at his coming. ²⁴ Then cometh the end, when he shall have delivered up the kingdom to God, even the Father, when he shall have put down all rule and all authority and power. ²⁵ For he must reign, till he hath put all enemies under his feet. ²⁶ The last enemy that shall be destroyed is death. ²⁷ For he hath put all things under his feet. But when he saith all things are put under him, it is manifest that he is excepted, which did put all things under him. ²⁸And when all things shall be subdued unto him, then shall the Son also himself be subject unto him that put all things under him, that God may be all in all.

²⁹ Else what shall they do which are baptized for the dead, if the dead rise not at all? Why are they then baptized for the dead?

³⁰And why stand we in jeopardy every hour? ³¹ I protest by your rejoicing which I have in Christ Jesus our Lord, I die daily. ³² If after the manner of men I have fought with beasts

at Ephesus, what advantageth it me, if the dead rise not? Let us eat and drink, for to morrow we die. ³³ Be not deceived: evil communications corrupt good manners. ³⁴Awake to righteousness, and sin not; for some have not the knowledge of God. I speak this to your shame. ³⁵ But some man will say, 'How are the dead raised up? And with what body do they come?' ³⁶ Thou fool, that which thou sowest is not quickened, except it die. ³⁷And that which thou sowest, thou sowest not that body that shall be, but bare grain, it may chance of wheat, or of some other grain, ³⁸ but God giveth it a body as it hath pleased him, and to every seed his own body. ³⁹All flesh is not the same flesh, but there is one kind of flesh of men, another flesh of beasts, another of fishes, and another of birds. ⁴⁰ There are also celestial bodies, and bodies terrestrial, but the glory of the celestial is one, and the glory of the terrestrial is another. ⁴¹ There is one glory of the sun, and another glory of the moon, and another glory of the stars, for one star differeth from another star in glory.

⁴² So also is the resurrection of the dead. It is sown in corruption; it is raised in incorruption. ⁴³ It is sown in dishonour; it is raised in glory. It is sown in weakness; it is raised in power. ⁴⁴ It is sown a natural body; it is raised a spiritual body. There is a natural body, and there is a spiritual body. ⁴⁵And so it is written, 'The first man Adam was made a living soul.' The last Adam was made a quickening spirit. ⁴⁶ Howbeit that was not first which is spiritual, but that which is natural; and afterward that which is spiritual. ⁴⁷ The first man is of the earth, earthy; the second man is the Lord from heaven. ⁴⁸As is the earthy, such are they also that are

earthy, and as is the heavenly, such are they also that are heavenly. ⁴⁹And as we have borne the image of the earthy, we shall also bear the image of the heavenly.

⁵⁰ Now this I say, brethren, that flesh and blood cannot inherit the kingdom of God; neither doth corruption inherit incorruption. ⁵¹Behold, I shew you a mystery. We shall not all sleep, but we shall all be changed, ⁵² in a moment, in the twinkling of an eye, at the last trump, for the trumpet shall sound, and the dead shall be raised incorruptible, and we shall be changed. ⁵³ For this corruptible must put on incorruption, and this mortal must put on immortality. ⁵⁴ So when this corruptible shall have put on incorruption, and this mortal shall have put on immortality, then shall be brought to pass the saying that is written, 'Death is swallowed up in victory.' ⁵⁵ O death, where is thy sting? O grave, where is thy victory? ⁵⁶ The sting of death is sin, and the strength of sin is the law. ⁵⁷ But thanks be to God, which giveth us the victory through our Lord Jesus Christ.

⁵⁸ Therefore, my beloved brethren, be ye stedfast, unmoveable, always abounding in the work of the Lord, forasmuch as ye know that your labour is not in vain in the Lord.

16 Now concerning the collection for the saints, as I have given order to the churches of Galatia, even so do ye. ² Upon the first day of the week let every one of you lay by him in store, as God hath prospered him, that there be no gatherings when I come. ³ And when I come, whomsoever ye shall approve by your letters, them will I send to bring your liberality unto Jerusalem. ⁴ And if it be meet that I go also, they shall go with me.

⁵ Now I will come unto you, when I shall pass through Macedonia, for I do pass through Macedonia. ⁶ And it may be that I will abide, yea, and winter with you, that ye may bring me on my journey whithersoever I go. ⁷ For I will not see you now by the way, but I trust to tarry a while with you, if the Lord permit. ⁸ But I will tarry at Ephesus until Pentecost. ⁹ For a great door and effectual is opened unto me, and there are many adversaries.

¹⁰ Now if Timotheus come, see that he may be with you without fear, for he worketh the work of the Lord, as I also do. ¹¹ Let no man therefore despise him, but conduct him forth in peace, that he may come unto me, for I look for him with the brethren.

¹² As touching our brother Apollos, I greatly desired him to come unto you with the brethren: but his will was not at all to come at this time; but he will come when he shall have convenient time.

¹³ Watch ye, stand fast in the faith, quit you like men, be strong. ¹⁴ Let all your things be done with charity.

¹⁵ I beseech you, brethren (ye know the house of Stephanas, that it is the firstfruits of Achaia, and that they have addicted themselves to the ministry of the saints), ¹⁶ that ye submit yourselves unto such, and to every one that helpeth with us, and laboureth. ¹⁷ I am glad of the coming of Stephanas and Fortunatus and Achaicus, for that which was lacking on your part they have supplied. ¹⁸ For they have refreshed my spirit and yours: therefore acknowledge ye them that are such.

¹⁹ The churches of Asia salute you. Aquila and Priscilla salute you much in the Lord, with the church that is in their house. ²⁰All the brethren greet you. Greet ye one another with an holy kiss.

²¹ The salutation of me Paul with mine own hand. ²² If any man love not the Lord Jesus Christ, let him be Anathema Maranatha. ²³ The grace of our Lord Jesus Christ be with you. ²⁴ My love be with you all in Christ Jesus. Amen.

the second epistle of paul the apostle to the corinthians

Paul, an apostle of Jesus Christ by the will of God, and Timothy our brother, unto the church of God which is at Corinth, with all the saints which are in all Achaia:

²Grace be to you and peace from God our Father, and from the Lord Jesus Christ.

³Blessed be God, even the Father of our Lord Jesus Christ, the Father of mercies, and the God of all comfort, ⁴who comforteth us in all our tribulation, that we may be able to comfort them which are in any trouble, by the comfort wherewith we ourselves are comforted of God. ⁵For as the sufferings of Christ abound in us, so our consolation also aboundeth by Christ. ⁶And whether we be afflicted, it is for your consolation and salvation, which is effectual in the enduring of the same sufferings which we also suffer; or whether we be comforted, it is for your consolation and salvation. ⁷And our hope of you is stedfast, knowing, that as ye are partakers of the sufferings, so shall ye be also of the consolation. ⁸For we would not, brethren, have you ignorant of our trouble which came to us in Asia, that we were pressed out of measure, above strength, insomuch that we despaired even of life: ⁹but we had the sentence of death in ourselves, that we should not trust in ourselves, but in God which raiseth the dead, ¹⁰who delivered us from so great a death, and doth deliver: in whom we trust that he will yet deliver us. ¹¹Ye also helping together by prayer

for us, that for the gift bestowed upon us by the means of many persons thanks may be given by many on our behalf.

¹² For our rejoicing is this, the testimony of our conscience, that in simplicity and godly sincerity, not with fleshly wisdom, but by the grace of God, we have had our conversation in the world, and more abundantly to you-ward. ¹³ For we write none other things unto you, than what ye read or acknowledge, and I trust ye shall acknowledge even to the end, ¹⁴ as also ye have acknowledged us in part, that we are your rejoicing, even as ye also are ours in the day of the Lord Jesus.

¹⁵ And in this confidence I was minded to come unto you before, that ye might have a second benefit, ¹⁶ and to pass by you into Macedonia, and to come again out of Macedonia unto you, and of you to be brought on my way toward Judaea. ¹⁷ When I therefore was thus minded, did I use lightness? Or the things that I purpose, do I purpose according to the flesh, that with me there should be yea yea, and nay nay? ¹⁸ But as God is true, our word toward you was not yea and nay. ¹⁹ For the Son of God, Jesus Christ, who was preached among you by us, even by me and Silvanus and Timotheus, was not yea and nay, but in him was yea. ²⁰ For all the promises of God in him are yea, and in him amen, unto the glory of God by us. ²¹ Now he which stablisheth us with you in Christ, and hath anointed us, is God, ²² who hath also sealed us, and given the earnest of the Spirit in our hearts.

²³ Moreover I call God for a record upon my soul, that to spare you I came not as yet unto Corinth. ²⁴ Not for that we have dominion over your faith, but are helpers of your joy, for by faith ye stand.

2 But I determined this with myself, that I would not come again to you in heaviness. ²For if I make you sorry, who is he then that maketh me glad, but the same which is made sorry by me? ³And I wrote this same unto you, lest, when I came, I should have sorrow from them of whom I ought to rejoice; having confidence in you all, that my joy is the joy of you all. ⁴For out of much affliction and anguish of heart I wrote unto you with many tears; not that ye should be grieved, but that ye might know the love which I have more abundantly unto you.

⁵But if any have caused grief, he hath not grieved me, but in part, that I may not overcharge you all. ⁶Sufficient to such a man is this punishment, which was inflicted of many. ⁷So that contrariwise ye ought rather to forgive him, and comfort him, lest perhaps such a one should be swallowed up with overmuch sorrow. ⁸Wherefore I beseech you that ye would confirm your love toward him. ⁹For to this end also did I write, that I might know the proof of you, whether ye be obedient in all things. ¹⁰To whom ye forgive any thing, I forgive also, for if I forgave any thing, to whom I forgave it, for your sakes forgave I it in the person of Christ, ¹¹lest Satan should get an advantage of us, for we are not ignorant of his devices.

¹²Furthermore, when I came to Troas to preach Christ's gospel, and a door was opened unto me of the Lord, ¹³I had no rest in my spirit, because I found not Titus my brother, but taking my leave of them, I went from thence into Macedonia.

¹⁴Now thanks be unto God, which always causeth us to triumph in Christ, and maketh manifest the savour of his knowledge by us in every place. ¹⁵For we are unto God a

sweet savour of Christ, in them that are saved, and in them that perish; ¹⁶ to the one we are the savour of death unto death; and to the other the savour of life unto life. And who is sufficient for these things? ¹⁷ For we are not as many, which corrupt the word of God, but as of sincerity, but as of God, in the sight of God speak we in Christ.

3 Do we begin again to commend ourselves? Or need we, as some others, epistles of commendation to you, or letters of commendation from you? ² Ye are our epistle written in our hearts, known and read of all men; ³ forasmuch as ye are manifestly declared to be the epistle of Christ ministered by us, written not with ink, but with the Spirit of the living God; not in tables of stone, but in fleshy tables of the heart.

⁴ And such trust have we through Christ to God-ward: ⁵ not that we are sufficient of ourselves to think any thing as of ourselves, but our sufficiency is of God, ⁶ who also hath made us able ministers of the new testament; not of the letter, but of the spirit; for the letter killeth, but the spirit giveth life.

⁷ But if the ministration of death, written and engraven in stones, was glorious, so that the children of Israel could not stedfastly behold the face of Moses for the glory of his countenance, which glory was to be done away. ⁸ How shall not the ministration of the spirit be rather glorious? ⁹ For if the ministration of condemnation be glory, much more doth the ministration of righteousness exceed in glory. ¹⁰ For even that which was made glorious had no glory in this respect, by reason of the glory that excelleth. ¹¹ For if that which is done away was glorious, much more that which remaineth is glorious.

¹² Seeing then that we have such hope, we use great plainness of speech, ¹³ and not as Moses, which put a vail over his face, that the children of Israel could not stedfastly look to the end of that which is abolished, ¹⁴ but their minds were blinded, for until this day remaineth the same vail untaken away in the reading of the old testament; which vail is done away in Christ. ¹⁵ But even unto this day, when Moses is read, the vail is upon their heart. ¹⁶ Nevertheless when it shall turn to the Lord, the vail shall be taken away. ¹⁷ Now the Lord is that Spirit, and where the Spirit of the Lord is, there is liberty. ¹⁸ But we all, with open face beholding as in a glass the glory of the Lord, are changed into the same image from glory to glory, even as by the Spirit of the Lord.

4 Therefore seeing we have this ministry, as we have received mercy, we faint not, ² but have renounced the hidden things of dishonesty, not walking in craftiness, nor handling the word of God deceitfully; but by manifestation of the truth commending ourselves to every man's conscience in the sight of God. ³ But if our gospel be hid, it is hid to them that are lost, ⁴ in whom the god of this world hath blinded the minds of them which believe not, lest the light of the glorious gospel of Christ, who is the image of God, should shine unto them. ⁵ For we preach not ourselves, but Christ Jesus the Lord; and ourselves your servants for Jesus' sake. ⁶ For God, who commanded the light to shine out of darkness, hath shined in our hearts, to give the light of the knowledge of the glory of God in the face of Jesus Christ.

⁷ But we have this treasure in earthen vessels, that the

excellency of the power may be of God, and not of us. ⁸ We are troubled on every side, yet not distressed; we are perplexed, but not in despair; ⁹ persecuted, but not forsaken; cast down, but not destroyed; ¹⁰ always bearing about in the body the dying of the Lord Jesus, that the life also of Jesus might be made manifest in our body. ¹¹ For we which live are alway delivered unto death for Jesus' sake, that the life also of Jesus might be made manifest in our mortal flesh. ¹² So then death worketh in us, but life in you. ¹³ We having the same spirit of faith, according as it is written, 'I believed, and therefore have I spoken'; we also believe, and therefore speak, ¹⁴ knowing that he which raised up the Lord Jesus shall raise up us also by Jesus, and shall present us with you. ¹⁵ For all things are for your sakes, that the abundant grace might through the thanksgiving of many redound to the glory of God.

¹⁶ For which cause we faint not; but though our outward man perish, yet the inward man is renewed day by day. ¹⁷ For our light affliction, which is but for a moment, worketh for us a far more exceeding and eternal weight of glory; ¹⁸ while we look not at the things which are seen, but at the things which are not seen: for the things which are seen are temporal, but the things which are not seen are eternal.

5 For we know that if our earthly house of this tabernacle were dissolved, we have a building of God, an house not made with hands, eternal in the heavens. ² For in this we groan, earnestly desiring to be clothed upon with our house which is from heaven, ³ if so be that being clothed we shall not be found naked. ⁴ For we that are in this tabernacle do

groan, being burdened, not for that we would be unclothed, but clothed upon, that mortality might be swallowed up of life. ⁵ Now he that hath wrought us for the selfsame thing is God, who also hath given unto us the earnest of the Spirit. ⁶ Therefore we are always confident, knowing that, whilst we are at home in the body, we are absent from the Lord ⁷(for we walk by faith, not by sight). ⁸ We are confident, I say, and willing rather to be absent from the body, and to be present with the Lord. ⁹ Wherefore we labour, that, whether present or absent, we may be accepted of him. ¹⁰ For we must all appear before the judgment seat of Christ; that every one may receive the things done in his body, according to that he hath done, whether it be good or bad. ¹¹ Knowing therefore the terror of the Lord, we persuade men; but we are made manifest unto God; and I trust also are made manifest in your consciences. ¹² For we commend not ourselves again unto you, but give you occasion to glory on our behalf, that ye may have somewhat to answer them which glory in appearance, and not in heart.

¹³ For whether we be beside ourselves, it is to God, or whether we be sober, it is for your cause. ¹⁴ For the love of Christ constraineth us, because we thus judge, that if one died for all, then were all dead, ¹⁵ and that he died for all, that they which live should not henceforth live unto themselves, but unto him which died for them, and rose again.

¹⁶ Wherefore henceforth know we no man after the flesh: yea, though we have known Christ after the flesh, yet now henceforth know we him no more. ¹⁷ Therefore if any man be in Christ, he is a new creature. Old things are passed away;

behold, all things are become new. [18]And all things are of God, who hath reconciled us to himself by Jesus Christ, and hath given to us the ministry of reconciliation; [19]to wit, that God was in Christ, reconciling the world unto himself, not imputing their trespasses unto them, and hath committed unto us the word of reconciliation. [20]Now then we are ambassadors for Christ, as though God did beseech you by us. We pray you in Christ's stead, be ye reconciled to God. [21]For he hath made him to be sin for us, who knew no sin, that we might be made the righteousness of God in him.

6 We then, as workers together with him, beseech you also that ye receive not the grace of God in vain. [2](For he saith, I have heard thee in a time accepted, and in the day of salvation have I succoured thee: behold, now is the accepted time; behold, now is the day of salvation.) [3]Giving no offence in any thing, that the ministry be not blamed, [4]but in all things approving ourselves as the ministers of God, in much patience, in afflictions, in necessities, in distresses, [5]in stripes, in imprisonments, in tumults, in labours, in watchings, in fastings; [6]by pureness, by knowledge, by longsuffering, by kindness, by the Holy Ghost, by love unfeigned, [7]by the word of truth, by the power of God, by the armour of righteousness on the right hand and on the left, [8]by honour and dishonour, by evil report and good report; as deceivers, and yet true; [9]as unknown, and yet well known; as dying, and, behold, we live; as chastened, and not killed; [10]as sorrowful, yet alway rejoicing; as poor, yet making many rich; as having nothing, and yet possessing all things. [11]O ye

Corinthians, our mouth is open unto you, our heart is enlarged. [12] Ye are not straitened in us, but ye are straitened in your own bowels. [13] Now for a recompence in the same (I speak as unto my children), be ye also enlarged.

[14] Be ye not unequally yoked together with unbelievers, for what fellowship hath righteousness with unrighteousness? And what communion hath light with darkness? [15] And what concord hath Christ with Belial? Or what part hath he that believeth with an infidel? [16] And what agreement hath the temple of God with idols? For ye are the temple of the living God, as God hath said, 'I will dwell in them, and walk in them; and I will be their God, and they shall be my people. [17] Wherefore come out from among them, and be ye separate,' saith the Lord, 'And touch not the unclean thing; and I will receive you, [18] and will be a Father unto you, and ye shall be my sons and daughters,' saith the Lord Almighty.

7 Having therefore these promises, dearly beloved, let us cleanse ourselves from all filthiness of the flesh and spirit, perfecting holiness in the fear of God.

[2] Receive us; we have wronged no man, we have corrupted no man, we have defrauded no man. [3] I speak not this to condemn you, for I have said before, that ye are in our hearts to die and live with you. [4] Great is my boldness of speech toward you, great is my glorying of you. I am filled with comfort, I am exceeding joyful in all our tribulation.

[5] For, when we were come into Macedonia, our flesh had no rest, but we were troubled on every side; without were fightings, within were fears. [6] Nevertheless God, that

comforteth those that are cast down, comforted us by the coming of Titus; [7]and not by his coming only, but by the consolation wherewith he was comforted in you, when he told us your earnest desire, your mourning, your fervent mind toward me; so that I rejoiced the more. [8]For though I made you sorry with a letter, I do not repent, though I did repent, for I perceive that the same epistle hath made you sorry, though it were but for a season. [9]Now I rejoice, not that ye were made sorry, but that ye sorrowed to repentance, for ye were made sorry after a godly manner, that ye might receive damage by us in nothing. [10]For godly sorrow worketh repentance to salvation not to be repented of, but the sorrow of the world worketh death. [11]For behold this selfsame thing, that ye sorrowed after a godly sort, what carefulness it wrought in you, yea, what clearing of yourselves, yea, what indignation, yea, what fear, yea, what vehement desire, yea, what zeal, yea, what revenge! In all things ye have approved yourselves to be clear in this matter. [12]Wherefore, though I wrote unto you, I did it not for his cause that had done the wrong, nor for his cause that suffered wrong, but that our care for you in the sight of God might appear unto you.

[13]Therefore we were comforted in your comfort; yea, and exceedingly the more joyed we for the joy of Titus, because his spirit was refreshed by you all. [14]For if I have boasted any thing to him of you, I am not ashamed, but as we spake all things to you in truth, even so our boasting, which I made before Titus, is found a truth. [15]And his inward affection is more abundant toward you, whilst he remembereth the obedience of you all, how with fear and trembling ye received him. [16]I

rejoice therefore that I have confidence in you in all things.

8 Moreover, brethren, we do you to wit of the grace of God bestowed on the churches of Macedonia; ²how that in a great trial of affliction the abundance of their joy and their deep poverty abounded unto the riches of their liberality. ³For to their power, I bear record, yea, and beyond their power they were willing of themselves, ⁴praying us with much intreaty that we would receive the gift, and take upon us the fellowship of the ministering to the saints. ⁵And this they did, not as we hoped, but first gave their own selves to the Lord, and unto us by the will of God. ⁶Insomuch that we desired Titus, that as he had begun, so he would also finish in you the same grace also. ⁷Therefore, as ye abound in every thing, in faith, and utterance, and knowledge, and in all diligence, and in your love to us, see that ye abound in this grace also.

⁸I speak not by commandment, but by occasion of the forwardness of others, and to prove the sincerity of your love. ⁹For ye know the grace of our Lord Jesus Christ, that, though he was rich, yet for your sakes he became poor, that ye through his poverty might be rich. ¹⁰And herein I give my advice, for this is expedient for you, who have begun before, not only to do, but also to be forward a year ago. ¹¹Now therefore perform the doing of it; that as there was a readiness to will, so there may be a performance also out of that which ye have. ¹²For if there be first a willing mind, it is accepted according to that a man hath, and not according to that he hath not. ¹³For I mean not that other men be eased, and ye

burdened, ¹⁴ But by an equality, that now at this time your abundance may be a supply for their want, that their abundance also may be a supply for your want, that there may be equality, ¹⁵ as it is written, 'He that had gathered much had nothing over; and he that had gathered little had no lack.' ¹⁶ But thanks be to God, which put the same earnest care into the heart of Titus for you. ¹⁷ For indeed he accepted the exhortation; but being more forward, of his own accord he went unto you. ¹⁸ And we have sent with him the brother, whose praise is in the gospel throughout all the churches; ¹⁹ and not that only, but who was also chosen of the churches to travel with us with this grace, which is administered by us to the glory of the same Lord, and declaration of your ready mind; ²⁰ avoiding this, that no man should blame us in this abundance which is administered by us; ²¹ providing for honest things, not only in the sight of the Lord, but also in the sight of men. ²² And we have sent with them our brother, whom we have oftentimes proved diligent in many things, but now much more diligent, upon the great confidence which I have in you. ²³ Whether any do enquire of Titus, he is my partner and fellowhelper concerning you; or our brethren be enquired of, they are the messengers of the churches, and the glory of Christ. ²⁴ Wherefore shew ye to them, and before the churches, the proof of your love, and of our boasting on your behalf.

9 For as touching the ministering to the saints, it is superfluous for me to write to you, ² for I know the forwardness of your mind, for which I boast of you to them of Macedonia, that Achaia was ready a year ago; and your zeal

hath provoked very many. ³ Yet have I sent the brethren, lest our boasting of you should be in vain in this behalf; that, as I said, ye may be ready, ⁴ lest haply if they of Macedonia come with me, and find you unprepared, we (that we say not, ye) should be ashamed in this same confident boasting. ⁵ Therefore I thought it necessary to exhort the brethren, that they would go before unto you, and make up beforehand your bounty, whereof ye had notice before, that the same might be ready, as a matter of bounty, and not as of covetousness. ⁶ But this I say: he which soweth sparingly shall reap also sparingly; and he which soweth bountifully shall reap also bountifully. ⁷ Every man according as he purposeth in his heart, so let him give, not grudgingly, or of necessity, for God loveth a cheerful giver. ⁸ And God is able to make all grace abound toward you, that ye, always having all sufficiency in all things, may abound to every good work: ⁹ (As it is written, 'He hath dispersed abroad; he hath given to the poor; his righteousness remaineth for ever.' ¹⁰ Now he that ministereth seed to the sower doth minister bread for your food, and multiply your seed sown, and increase the fruits of your righteousness.) ¹¹ Being enriched in every thing to all bountifulness, which causeth through us thanksgiving to God. ¹² For the administration of this service not only supplieth the want of the saints, but is abundant also by many thanksgivings unto God; ¹³ whiles by the experiment of this ministration they glorify God for your professed subjection unto the gospel of Christ, and for your liberal distribution unto them, and unto all men, ¹⁴ and by their prayer for you, which long after you for the exceeding grace of

God in you. ¹⁵ Thanks be unto God for his unspeakable gift.

10 Now I Paul myself beseech you by the meekness and gentleness of Christ, who in presence am base among you, but being absent am bold toward you, ² but I beseech you, that I may not be bold when I am present with that confidence, wherewith I think to be bold against some, which think of us as if we walked according to the flesh. ³ For though we walk in the flesh, we do not war after the flesh ⁴(for the weapons of our warfare are not carnal, but mighty through God to the pulling down of strong holds), ⁵casting down imaginations, and every high thing that exalteth itself against the knowledge of God, and bringing into captivity every thought to the obedience of Christ; ⁶ and having in a readiness to revenge all disobedience, when your obedience is fulfilled.

⁷ Do ye look on things after the outward appearance? If any man trust to himself that he is Christ's, let him of himself think this again, that, as he is Christ's, even so are we Christ's. ⁸ For though I should boast somewhat more of our authority, which the Lord hath given us for edification, and not for your destruction, I should not be ashamed, ⁹ that I may not seem as if I would terrify you by letters. ¹⁰ For 'His letters,' say they, 'are weighty and powerful; but his bodily presence is weak, and his speech contemptible.' ¹¹ Let such an one think this, that, such as we are in word by letters when we are absent, such will we be also in deed when we are present.

¹² For we dare not make ourselves of the number, or compare ourselves with some that commend themselves, but they measuring themselves by themselves, and comparing

themselves among themselves, are not wise. ¹³ But we will not boast of things without our measure, but according to the measure of the rule which God hath distributed to us, a measure to reach even unto you. ¹⁴ For we stretch not ourselves beyond our measure, as though we reached not unto you, for we are come as far as to you also in preaching the gospel of Christ, ¹⁵ not boasting of things without our measure, that is, of other men's labours; but having hope, when your faith is increased, that we shall be enlarged by you according to our rule abundantly, ¹⁶ to preach the gospel in the regions beyond you, and not to boast in another man's line of things made ready to our hand. ¹⁷ But he that glorieth, let him glory in the Lord. ¹⁸ For not he that commendeth himself is approved, but whom the Lord commendeth.

11 Would to God ye could bear with me a little in my folly, and indeed bear with me. ² For I am jealous over you with godly jealousy, for I have espoused you to one husband, that I may present you as a chaste virgin to Christ. ³ But I fear, lest by any means, as the serpent beguiled Eve through his subtilty, so your minds should be corrupted from the simplicity that is in Christ. ⁴ For if he that cometh preacheth another Jesus, whom we have not preached, or if ye receive another spirit, which ye have not received, or another gospel, which ye have not accepted, ye might well bear with him. ⁵ For I suppose I was not a whit behind the very chiefest apostles. ⁶ But though I be rude in speech, yet not in knowledge; but we have been throughly made manifest among you in all things.

⁷ Have I committed an offence in abasing myself that ye might be exalted, because I have preached to you the gospel of God freely? ⁸ I robbed other churches, taking wages of them, to do you service. ⁹ And when I was present with you, and wanted, I was chargeable to no man, for that which was lacking to me the brethren which came from Macedonia supplied, and in all things I have kept myself from being burdensome unto you, and so will I keep myself. ¹⁰ As the truth of Christ is in me, no man shall stop me of this boasting in the regions of Achaia. ¹¹ Wherefore? Because I love you not? God knoweth.

¹² But what I do, that I will do, that I may cut off occasion from them which desire occasion; that wherein they glory, they may be found even as we. ¹³ For such are false apostles, deceitful workers, transforming themselves into the apostles of Christ. ¹⁴ And no marvel; for Satan himself is transformed into an angel of light. ¹⁵ Therefore it is no great thing if his ministers also be transformed as the ministers of righteousness, whose end shall be according to their works.

¹⁶ I say again, let no man think me a fool; if otherwise, yet as a fool receive me, that I may boast myself a little. ¹⁷ That which I speak, I speak it not after the Lord, but as it were foolishly, in this confidence of boasting. ¹⁸ Seeing that many glory after the flesh, I will glory also. ¹⁹ For ye suffer fools gladly, seeing ye yourselves are wise. ²⁰ For ye suffer, if a man bring you into bondage, if a man devour you, if a man take of you, if a man exalt himself, if a man smite you on the face. ²¹ I speak as concerning reproach, as though we had been weak. Howbeit where-

insoever any is bold (I speak foolishly), I am bold also.

²²Are they Hebrews? So am I. Are they Israelites? So am I. Are they the seed of Abraham? So am I. ²³Are they ministers of Christ? (I speak as a fool.) I am more; in labours more abundant, in stripes above measure, in prisons more frequent, in deaths oft. ²⁴Of the Jews five times received I forty stripes save one. ²⁵Thrice was I beaten with rods, once was I stoned, thrice I suffered shipwreck, a night and a day I have been in the deep; ²⁶in journeyings often, in perils of waters, in perils of robbers, in perils by mine own countrymen, in perils by the heathen, in perils in the city, in perils in the wilderness, in perils in the sea, in perils among false brethren; ²⁷in weariness and painfulness, in watchings often, in hunger and thirst, in fastings often, in cold and nakedness. ²⁸Beside those things that are without, that which cometh upon me daily, the care of all the churches. ²⁹Who is weak, and I am not weak? Who is offended, and I burn not? ³⁰If I must needs glory, I will glory of the things which concern mine infirmities. ³¹The God and Father of our Lord Jesus Christ, which is blessed for evermore, knoweth that I lie not. ³²In Damascus the governor under Aretas the king kept the city of the Damascenes with a garrison, desirous to apprehend me, ³³and through a window in a basket was I let down by the wall, and escaped his hands.

12 It is not expedient for me doubtless to glory. I will come to visions and revelations of the Lord. ²I knew a man in Christ above fourteen years ago (whether in the body, I cannot tell; or whether out of the body, I cannot tell;

God knoweth), such an one caught up to the third heaven. ³And I knew such a man (whether in the body, or out of the body, I cannot tell; God knoweth); ⁴how that he was caught up into paradise, and heard unspeakable words, which it is not lawful for a man to utter. ⁵Of such an one will I glory; yet of myself I will not glory, but in mine infirmities. ⁶For though I would desire to glory, I shall not be a fool; for I will say the truth; but now I forbear, lest any man should think of me above that which he seeth me to be, or that he heareth of me. ⁷And lest I should be exalted above measure through the abundance of the revelations, there was given to me a thorn in the flesh, the messenger of Satan to buffet me, lest I should be exalted above measure. ⁸For this thing I besought the Lord thrice, that it might depart from me. ⁹And he said unto me, 'My grace is sufficient for thee, for my strength is made perfect in weakness.' Most gladly therefore will I rather glory in my infirmities, that the power of Christ may rest upon me. ¹⁰Therefore I take pleasure in infirmities, in reproaches, in necessities, in persecutions, in distresses for Christ's sake, for when I am weak, then am I strong.

¹¹I am become a fool in glorying; ye have compelled me, for I ought to have been commended of you, for in nothing am I behind the very chiefest apostles, though I be nothing. ¹²Truly the signs of an apostle were wrought among you in all patience, in signs, and wonders, and mighty deeds. ¹³For what is it wherein ye were inferior to other churches, except it be that I myself was not burdensome to you? Forgive me this wrong.

¹⁴Behold, the third time I am ready to come to you; and I

will not be burdensome to you, for I seek not yours, but you, for the children ought not to lay up for the parents, but the parents for the children. ¹⁵And I will very gladly spend and be spent for you; though the more abundantly I love you, the less I be loved. ¹⁶But be it so, I did not burden you; nevertheless, being crafty, I caught you with guile. ¹⁷Did I make a gain of you by any of them whom I sent unto you? ¹⁸I desired Titus, and with him I sent a brother. Did Titus make a gain of you? Walked we not in the same spirit? Walked we not in the same steps?

¹⁹Again, think ye that we excuse ourselves unto you? We speak before God in Christ, but we do all things, dearly beloved, for your edifying. ²⁰For I fear, lest, when I come, I shall not find you such as I would, and that I shall be found unto you such as ye would not: lest there be debates, envyings, wraths, strifes, backbitings, whisperings, swellings, tumults; ²¹and lest, when I come again, my God will humble me among you, and that I shall bewail many which have sinned already, and have not repented of the uncleanness and fornication and lasciviousness which they have committed.

13 This is the third time I am coming to you. In the mouth of two or three witnesses shall every word be established. ²I told you before, and foretell you, as if I were present, the second time; and being absent now I write to them which heretofore have sinned, and to all other, that, if I come again, I will not spare, ³since ye seek a proof of Christ speaking in me, which to you-ward is not weak, but is mighty in you. ⁴For though he was crucified through weakness, yet he

liveth by the power of God. For we also are weak in him, but we shall live with him by the power of God toward you.

⁵Examine yourselves, whether ye be in the faith; prove your own selves. Know ye not your own selves, how that Jesus Christ is in you, except ye be reprobates? ⁶But I trust that ye shall know that we are not reprobates. ⁷Now I pray to God that ye do no evil; not that we should appear approved, but that ye should do that which is honest, though we be as reprobates. ⁸For we can do nothing against the truth, but for the truth. ⁹For we are glad, when we are weak, and ye are strong, and this also we wish, even your perfection. ¹⁰Therefore I write these things being absent, lest being present I should use sharpness, according to the power which the Lord hath given me to edification, and not to destruction.

¹¹Finally, brethren, farewell. Be perfect, be of good comfort, be of one mind, live in peace; and the God of love and peace shall be with you. ¹²Greet one another with an holy kiss. ¹³All the saints salute you. ¹⁴The grace of the Lord Jesus Christ, and the love of God, and the communion of the Holy Ghost, be with you all. Amen.

Condescend